All These Roads
The Poetry of Louis Dudek

All These Roads

The Poetry of Louis Dudek

Selected
with an
introduction by
Karis Shearer
and an
afterword by
Frank Davey

LAURIER POETRY SERIES

Wilfrid Laurier University Press

We acknowledge the support of the Canada Council for the Arts for our publishing program. We acknowledge the financial support of the Government of Canada through the Book Publishing Industry Development Program for our publishing activities.

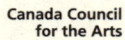 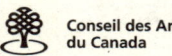 

Library and Archives Canada Cataloguing in Publication

Dudek, Louis, 1918–2001.
  All these roads : the poetry of Louis Dudek / selected with an introduction by Karis Shearer ; and an afterword by Frank Davey.

(Laurier poetry series)
Includes bibliographical references.
ISBN 978-1-55458-039-2

  I. Shearer, Karis, 1980–   II. Title.   III. Series.

PS8507.U43A64 2008   C811'.54   C2008-900620-8

Table of Contents

Long Poems

Foreword

At the beginning of the twenty-first century, poetry in Canada—writing and publishing it, reading and thinking about it—finds itself in a strangely conflicted place. We have many strong poets continuing to produce exciting new work, and there is still a small audience for poetry; but increasingly, poetry is becoming a vulnerable art, for reasons that don't need to be rehearsed.

But there are things to be done: we need more real engagement with our poets. There needs to be more access to their work in more venues—in classrooms, in the public arena, in the media—and there needs to be more, and more different kinds, of publications that make the wide range of our contemporary poetry more widely available.

The hope that animates this series from Wilfrid Laurier University Press is that these volumes help to create and sustain the larger readership that contemporary Canadian poetry so richly deserves. Like our fiction writers, our poets are much celebrated abroad; they should just as properly be better known at home.

Our idea is to ask a critic (sometimes herself a poet) to select thirty-five poems from across a poet's career; write an engaging, accessible introduction; and have the poet write an afterword. In this way, we think that the usual practice of teaching a poet through eight or twelve poems from an anthology is much improved upon; and readers in and out of classrooms will have more useful, engaging, and comprehensive introductions to a poet's work. Readers might also come to see more readily, we hope, the connections among, as well as the distances between, the life and the work.

It was the ending of an Al Purdy poem that gave Margaret Laurence the epigraph for *The Diviners*: "but they had their being once / and left a place to stand on." Our poets still do, and they are leaving many places to stand on. We hope that this series helps, variously, to show how and why this is so.

—*Neil Besner*
General Editor

Biographical Note

As a poet, editor, anthologist, publisher, critic, translator, and professor, Louis Dudek was one of Canada's most important and influential cultural workers. Dudek was born in Montreal, February 6, 1918. He graduated from McGill University with a BA in English and History and, after working briefly as an advertising copywriter and freelance journalist, left for the United States to pursue graduate work at Columbia University, where he completed a PhD dissertation entitled "The Relations between Literature and the Press" (later published as *Literature and the Press*) and began a rigorous correspondence with Ezra Pound. In 1951, Dudek returned from New York to the city of his birth in order to take up a position as professor of English at McGill, where he became a renowned lecturer. His return to Canada marked the beginning of Dudek's efforts to revolutionize the Montreal poetry scene through little magazines and small-press publishing, providing alternatives to commercial presses for young poets. He became involved in several little magazines, including *First Statement* and *Contact* (with Raymond Souster), founded the little magazines *CIV/n* and *Delta* (1957–66), and in 1956 started *The McGill Poetry Series* (which gave a start to several young poets, including Leonard Cohen). He was also involved in founding Contact Press, Delta Canada, and DC Books.

Dudek's early poetry was published in *The McGill Daily*, the *Quebec Chronicle Telegraph*, *First Statement*, and *Northern Review*. His major volumes of poetry include *East of the City* (1946), *Twenty-four Poems* (1952), *The Searching Image* (1952), *Europe* (1954), *The Transparent Sea* (1956), *En México* (1958), *Laughing Stalks* (1958), *Atlantis* (1967), *Collected Poetry* (1971), *Selected Poems* (1979), *Poems from Atlantis* (1980), *Cross-Section* (1980), *Continuation I* (1981), *Zembla's Rocks* (1986), *Continuation II* (1990), *Small Perfect Things* (1991), *The Caged Tiger* (1997), and *The Surface of Time* (2000). Two important collections of Dudek's poetry have also been published: *The Poetry of Louis Dudek* (1998) and *Infinite Worlds* (1988), selected and edited by the poet Robin Blaser. A collection of essays commemorating Louis Dudek, *Eternal Conversations*, was published after his death in 2001.

Introduction

A major figure in Canadian modernism, Louis Dudek began his poetic career experimenting with the shorter imagist poem before producing what Robin Blaser has called "some of the most extraordinary long poems in the modern canon" (7). It was long poems like *Europe* (1954), *En México* (1958), *Atlantis* (1967), the *Continuation* poems *I* and *II*, along with Dudek's magazine and small-press work, that prompted critics to identify him as a significant bridge between two generations of Canadian poets: modernist and postmodern writers (Davey 7; Norris 120; Stromberg-Stein 116; Trehearne 262). Critical studies have explored Dudek's poetics of accumulation and encyclopedic scope (Trehearne), the lyric development of his long poems (Ruiz Sánchez), biographical aspects of his poetry (Stromberg-Stein), and the significance of his cultural work for Canadian modernism (Tremblay 2001). Ultimately, Dudek's is very much a poetry of ideas; deeply philosophical in nature, it reflects a consistent belief in purposeful art (as opposed to art for art's sake) and a persistent inquiry into the conditions of contemporary culture.

Functional Poetry

Dudek's mature poetics are best explained in a manifesto he wrote in the form of a poem-essay, titled "Functional Poetry: A Proposal." Published in his own *Delta* magazine in 1959, "Functional Poetry" begins by lamenting

> the *loss of ground to prose*   over the centuries
> *in the subject matter of poetry,*
> and the loss of freshness in method
> as the residue of "poetic" substance
> became fossilized in decadent metre and form (my italics)

In order to combat this loss, Dudek, in a call that reflects his lifelong belief in a poetry that adapts in order to influence the conditions of contemporary life, urges poets to produce work that is both "relevant" and "immediate," rather than the "iambic rhymed poetry" that "invites padding and distortion of the language, even in the best of hands" ("Metrics" 112); "[a] poem, after all, is not," Dudek reminds us, "something poured into prepared muffin tins" (113). Metre, he felt, was stale and constraining, preventing poetry from adapting to effectively perform its cultural work; furthermore, metre contributed to the decay or "loss of freshness in method," "mak[ing] it easy to counterfeit poetry; with the new method each poem is an original piece of music" (114).

Over the centuries, poets have routinely intervened in the mediation and theorization of their own art, and according to Dudek they "make the best critics, really the only lasting critics" ("Questions" 33). In this he echoes the likes of Ben Jonson, who maintained that "To judge of Poets is only the faculty of Poets" (642), and John Dryden, who contended that "Poets themselves are the most proper, though I conclude not the only, critics" (13). But in "Functional Poetry" it is not simply that a poet can act as a critic, but that poetry can and should act as a mode of criticism. In order to regain ground lost to prose in that regard, poetry must take on the work more often associated with prose, tasks that can include, but are not limited to, criticism, theory, philosophy, exposition, discourse, and review. "Write," Dudek commands, "whatever you write (for print, or letters) / not as prose, but as rhythmic poetry / (you will find the way)." Thus, in his insistence on investing poetry with the critical function of prose, Dudek would likely have taken Dryden's view one step further and rephrased it as "*Poetry* itself is the most proper, though I conclude not the only, mode of criticism."

As was no doubt intended, the experimental manifesto sparked a flurry of responses, many of which were printed—likely as excerpts from larger letters, though that much is unclear—in the subsequent issue of *Delta*. Some, like Z.A. Melzak, took up Dudek's call and responded in the form of a poem (12); others declared their support rather more bluntly: "I sincerely hope," wrote Jean Arsenault, "that your *Proposal* sinks into many of the fatheads in the poetry field" (11). And there were, of course, those who disagreed entirely: Goodridge MacDonald, for example, wrote in to say that Dudek's "functional poetry rather repel[led] [him]. Poetry has no function, no purpose. Like all forms of art, it simply is" (12). Both Dorothy Livesay and Eli Mandel were measured supporters of the proposal, Livesay admitting that Dudek's "experiment in talk—and the idea behind it" was one that she subscribed to, and Mandel agreeing that Dudek had put his thumb on the problem of poetry's loss of ground to prose. But each offered other possible solutions, including theatre, myth, and metaphor, as means of regaining that ground. When Mandel in his letter presses Dudek about what the content of his proposed functional poetry ought to be, Dudek as editor stays true to his manifesto and replies "[*The only thing to do is to answer Eli with poetry—next time. This has been too much prose. Any offers?*]" (13; original italics).

While critics have attributed Dudek's "functional poetry" thesis to the late fifties (Blaser 22; Goldie 31), when it was published, evidence from his correspondence with the American poet Ezra Pound shows that, in fact, the concerns that inform the essay "Functional Poetry" were expressed on paper nearly a decade earlier. Dudek had therefore developed his thesis *before* publishing *Europe* (1954), *The Transparent Sea* (1956), *En México* (1958), and *Laughing Stalks* (1958), not after, as critics have supposed. Not only do the thematic concerns of "Functional Poetry" begin to appear in Dudek's letters, but the formal tensions between poetry and prose are acted out as the letters develop. Initially, the mostly typewritten letters to Pound (beginning 26 May 1949) featured tidy prose paragraphs, the text justified smartly against left-hand margins. By early 1951, however, he had abandoned the left-hand margin entirely, with lines beginning to vary in length, and by 1952 he had begun to play with the spacing between both words and lines, dramatically varying line length, and effectively producing poem-letters of the kind described in his future program of poetics: "some form of improvised rhythmed speech / which is divided and shaped / by the run-on and end-stop system / of nota-tion." Finally, in a 12 November 1952 letter to Ezra Pound that strongly resem-bles the published version of the manifesto, Dudek produces a poem-letter that traces the same literary history as "Functional Poetry," ending with the following proposal:

> But then, one hasn't won back the ground
>   lost by the finger-nail clippers.   This, too, this jump,
>   is on the line of the reform   perpetuated by ACADEMIES.
>
>
>   Posit:
>   Mackerel crowded seas[1]   (a figure
>   for a kind of style)
>   and
>   a single pike in clear stream
>   (the other style)
>   Maybe the answer is   poetry??   i.e. poetry to
>   take over from prose,   the whole job?

Here, Dudek euphemistically attributes poetry's loss of ground to "the finger-nail clippers"—to the "artist [who], like the God of the creation, remains within or behind or above his handiwork, invisible, refined out of existence, indifferent, paring his fingernails" (Joyce 215). He refers, of course, to Stephen Dedalus's discussion of art and aesthetics with his friend Lynch, in Joyce's

Portrait of the Artist as a Young Man. Dudek then juxtaposes two figurative styles; the "mackerel crowded seas" (12) (likely a fecund symbolist poetry) of Yeats's "Sailing to Byzantium" and the "single pike in clear stream" (probably imagist poetry, like Pound's "In a Station of the Metro") might have the ability, he speculates, to counteract the damage done by the remote and indifferent poet.

Cultural Worker

In the 1950s, after his return to Montreal, Dudek involved himself—as professor, editor, anthologist, publisher, and critic—in virtually all aspects of poetic production, reception, and dissemination. Reflecting on the significance of Dudek's contributions to Canadian literature, Ken Norris once declared that he "created an entire environment for poetry to exist where once there was only a vacuum" (122). Though there were certainly poet-critics like A.J.M. Smith before him, Dudek, as Frank Davey has noted, is "the first to follow Arnold and Pound in combining poetry, criticism, polemic editing, and cultural criticism into one multi-faceted cultural vision" ("Introduction" 7). Not surprisingly, the work associated with each of those roles is enacted within Dudek's poetry itself, as much as it is carried out beyond the physical poetry text (as it was in the McGill University classroom, *Delta* and *CIV/n* magazines, critical articles, and anthologies).

Dudek was a passionate teacher throughout his life, both in the classroom at McGill—where a major teaching award is now named after him—and in the everyday spaces of his life. Upon inheriting the course "Great Writings of Europe" (still taught at McGill today), he "made it a study of literature in translation" ("Preface" 10). The affinities between "Great Writings of Europe" and his long poem *Europe* suggest that teaching became an extension of Dudek's writing and vice versa:

> On the whole I see the author reduced to a degraded position, brought to impotence by commercial and technological developments; and this has to do with the general degradation of civilized values that accompanies the evolution of historical ideas from about 1750 to present, that is, the content of "The Great Writings of Europe." ("Preface" 13)

Just as Dudek the poet makes his way into the classroom, Dudek the professor often makes his way into the poems, whether as a poet commenting on the profession (as in "What We Profess" or "The Retired Professor") or as a poet in the didactic mode (see especially his epigrams and the poem "Lesson"). The role of the teacher was one Dudek inhabited ubiquitously. "Louis," fellow poet

D.G. Jones has commented, "will teach you what he's found out about particle physics in the middle of a birthday party!" (118). The role is not far from that of mentor, and Dudek was certainly both to many poets and young scholars.

In "Advice to a Young Poet," Dudek assumes a mentor-persona who counsels: "there is no sudden reward. Publication through established presses is vanity. These are the real vanity presses. It is humility to publish privately, at your own cost." Dudek understood that in order for a young or new poet to break into the established scene, she often had to take matters into her own hands. Major presses represented commercial interests, tending to cater to popular taste and to be reluctant to take risks on experimental writing. With publication in large commercial presses often came a degree of popularity or fame, and from fame—so the logic goes—follows vanity. The humble and necessary alternative, then, is to turn to writer-run small-press publishing or to publish oneself, for "the real development [in literature] can only take place in the hands of real writers, i.e. in places like [*Open Letter*], or the Véhicule books in Montreal, or the new writing groups in the mid-west, or *Capilano* and *Antigonish Review*" (Dudek "Questions" 31). In this sense, Dudek encouraged and carried on the international avant-garde practice of creating venues and producing reception for one's own radical work—a type of intervention practised most notably by Ezra Pound, Tristan Tzara, and Hugo Ball in the earlier part of the twentieth century.

One of those venues was the McGill Poetry Series, which Dudek established in 1955 and funded mostly out his own pocket. The series published talented young poets like Seymour Mayne, Daryl Hine, David Solway, and Leonard Cohen. Though Cohen had been writing poetry before he met Dudek at McGill, it was Dudek who published him first in *CIV/n* 4. Cohen remembers the poet-publisher as "a legend for me—and an important figure at a certain moment in my life," a mentor whose "greatest contribution to Canadian writing is his sense of responsibility" (96). However, as Cohen's career drew him more and more into the spotlight of popular culture, Dudek's support for the poet waned, culminating in the article "Patterns in Recent Canadian Poetry," in which Dudek expresses the conflict and disappointment he felt toward his former protégé. Cohen, Dudek argued, belonged to a group of poets who grasped at "obscure cosmological imagery ... a confusion of symbolic images, often a rag-bag of classical mythology, in an effort to organize a chaos too large for them" (109); however, the poem "A Note for Leonard Cohen," included in this volume, reflects more ambivalently on Cohen's potential relationship to his Montreal mentors. For Dudek, good literature is always at odds with popular taste. In "Old Books," "the failed poems of long ago ... forgotten, like party dresses of youth," are relegated to the shelves to collect dust while new poets try their hand at the art in spite of a public who "prefers the ghost of Presley / and worships that fat calf."

The McGill Poetry Series was just one of a number of Dudek's efforts to create and build a poetic community. Another was the "Poetry Grapevine" he began while living in New York City, in which the poets involved (including Ezra Pound, William Carlos Williams, Charles Olson, and Raymond Souster) would contribute poems and comment on the poetry of others (Davey 10). In Dudek's work we see evidence of a mind that was constantly assessing, engaging, and challenging the world (especially the literary world) around him; in keeping with his belief in "functional poetry," he used his poems to do much of that work. These efforts at community-building manifest themselves in Dudek's poetry through the intertextual references and dedications that bring poets (in absentia) into literary conversation and debate. As he explains in his preface to the 1991 edition of *Europe*, "when I refer in my poems to philosophers and political thinkers (or other poets), it is not to echo their ideas, but rather because I have thought much and long, in my solitudes, using their thoughts as props and occasional gleams to illuminate the darkness" (9). This intertextuality also serves to dramatize debates that were raging, both in print and in person, in the literary scenes at the time. Dudek's love of debate is recollected here by three of his close friends and fellow poets (to whom several of his poems are dedicated)—Ron Everson, Ralph Gustafson, and F.R. Scott:

> One thing that makes him different is that he doesn't mind taking an opposing view. In fact, he perhaps takes to it a little quicker than most people. Most people want an agreeable conversation, he prefers having a good argument. (Everson 99)

> I always thoroughly, deeply enjoyed being in contact with him, and talking not only on the technique of poetry but more to simply exchange minds and Louis' greatest love is to argue.... He's a very erudite fellow. (Gustafson 105)

> What I like about his ideas is that he is not afraid to swim against the current.... He's not afraid to speak up and state his opinion. (Scott 123)

That lively spirit of debate is recorded in the satirical "Reply to Envious Arthur," in which Dudek directly refutes A.J.M. ("Arthur") Smith, in the tradition of the response poem that dates back to the Middle Ages and includes the work of such diverse pairs as Sir Walter Raleigh and Christopher Marlowe, Kenneth Koch and William Carlos Williams, and F.R. Scott and E.J. Pratt.[2] "Reply to Envious Arthur" shows Dudek's skill at the rhyming couplet, his sharp wit, as well as his playfulness and humour, as he engages his poetic rival. Commenting on his reply to Smith, Dudek writes, "It may surprise some readers to learn that I am and always have been an admirer of A.J.M. Smith's poetry. The kind of duel among poets is largely an exercise in poetic skills, and I am sure that Smith's couplets were written in the same spirit. One does smart, of course, under the snap of wit, and I was provoked. But later I wrote a newspaper piece under the title "A.J.M. Smith, Aesthetic Master of Canadian Poetry" (in *The Poetry of Louis Dudek* 99).

Dudek's poems also serve to negotiate the reception of his poetry, notably calling into question the notion of the critic (or poet, for that matter) as definitive interpreter of a given work. "*Europe*, At Sea" reports and mediates the reception, both positive and negative, of Dudek's first attempt at the long poem; at the risk of being redundant, one might say that the poem reviews the reviews. In "Hellcats in Heaven (Report on the book *Cerberus*)," for example, the poet imagines the reactions of four long-dead European poets—William Blake, Arthur Rimbaud, François Villon, and François Rabelais—to the volume he, Raymond Souster, and Irving Layton self-published in 1952. Each of the four hellcats' comments makes reference to his own poetry: the fifteenth-century French poet François Villon, for example, condemns the Cerberus poets to be hanged, the fate of the subjects of his own best-known poem, "La ballade des pendus." In a paradox reminiscent of Cohen's own *Beautiful Losers*, the Hellcats' damnation of the book *Cerberus* is actually high praise. These and other poems show that critical conversations about poetry can happen just as often within poems as in prose essays, and remind us of Friedrich Schlegel's conviction that "[p]oetry can only be criticized through poetry. A critique which is not itself a work of art, either in content as representation in the process of creation, or through its beautiful form and in the liberal tone in the spirit of the old Roman satire, has no right of citizenship within the realm of art" (132). Dudek would almost certainly have agreed.

His involvement with both the material and philosophical aspects of the poetic process allowed Dudek to create a consistent vision of modern poetry, making him "one of the great cultural architects of the twentieth century" (Tremblay 2005, 170), and, according to Robin Blaser, "Canada's most important—that is to say, consequential—modern voice" (9). Although some have cast doubt on Dudek's importance to Canadian literature (Goldie 51), he has been recognized repeatedly for setting an important precedent effecting cultural change through the unification of his poetry and his extra-poetic work. In 1980, Frank Davey suggested that Dudek's "long poems, the first major modernist long poems in Canadian literature, open up formal possibilities which are later to dominate important work by Marlatt, Bowering, Nichol,

Lee, and Kroetsch" ("Introduction" 7); I would now suggest that Dudek's experimental essay-poems, small-press publishing, and little-magazine editing also opened up the way for those five poets' cultural work—work that would resemble Dudek's in its desire to gather together a community and advance a marginal poetics alongside a particular cultural vision.

Long Poems

With his first major attempt at the longer form, *Europe* (1954), Dudek departs significantly from the established tradition of long poems in Canada, which, up until that point, had been predominantly narrative in kind. *Europe* was far more lyrical and fragmented than a poem like E.J. Pratt's *Towards the Last Spike*, published just three years earlier:

> Tired of the midnight toss, lock-jawed with yawns,
> He left the bed and, shuffling to the window,
> He opened it. The air would cool him off
> And sooth his shoulder burns. He felt his ribs:
> Strange, nothing broken—how those crazy drowses
> Had made the fictions tangle with the facts! (219)

Compare this to Dudek's willingness to depart from the left-hand margin, to work in a looser and more impressionistic form in fragment 59 of *Europe*:

> Where the sea smashes
> on the rocks at Bordighera:
> simply for pleasure,
>   like the surf at Sete,
>   alone, for miles and miles
>
> a strip of land, where there is water on both sides
> and a good road running by the sea—
> lonely, we stopped and stripped
> for the sweet salt surf, the sea
> that took us in as though we were nothing
>   (making that poem)

And compare fragment 59 to this passage from the third book of bp Nichol's *The Martyrology* (1976):

> one ocean which is all oceans holy
> remember my father's words
> having driven from pacific to atlantic

"my god we're a long way from home"
return to that water   salt in our gills   it fills us

hands together in the sun

breathe in   breathe out

alokanorée

aloka norée (np)

Like *Europe*, *The Martyrology* expresses an encyclopedic impulse to compile
pieces of the poet's consciousness, including parts of passing conversations
("'Just a lot of water,'" someone says in the early pages of *Europe*), bodily
rhythms of the breath, and limited visual perceptions of the landscape sur-
rounding the poet. Further linking these two passages is the symbol of the sea,
which for *Europe* is the poem's central symbol, as the jungle is to *En México*.
Though the sea in *Europe* serves as a symbol for artistic creation, it is also, on
a more practical level, that which facilitates Dudek and his wife Stephanie's
voyage to Europe.

Whether literal or figurative, the voyage lies at the heart of all of Dudek's
long poems, from *Europe* to *Atlantis* to the *Continuations*; for the poet, it is
both the impetus for and the subject of poetry. In the paper he delivered at
the 1983 Long Liners Conference, Dudek explains: "The real subject of the
long poem is a search, the search for a truth of personal being and experience
such as poetry has never been privileged to explore. It is a voyage in a new
found land" (85). Though this might seem like a sweeping, idealistic state-
ment, the speaker in *Atlantis* proclaims: "'I hate travel.' / But all poetry I've
ever written seems to be about travel. / Like this voyage … (all life's a voyage /
and any small voyage is a lifetime in a little)" (9–10). Travel is never straight-
forward, as the speaker here is aware in his moment of self-reflection and
ambivalence. It is only one of many such moments in the long poems (par-
ticularly *En México*) that draw attention to the poet's complex relationship
with travel, as well as to the traveller's multifarious and uneasy relationship
with the land he is visiting, with its people, their history and their culture.
From Dudek's "Functional Poetry," this volume's title, *All These Roads*,
gestures toward these complexities in a figurative way:

All these roads (of mod po)
converge in a single purpose
        to write it as they write prose
Lots of it, on all subjects that call
            for communication

Though Dudek was often didactic, he was never prescriptive; he recognized that poetry had a job to do, but also that many voices would speak and many roads would be taken. Most importantly, he saw that the task must be a communal effort. "Anyone who travels," he wrote in *Atlantis*, "sees others at the crossroads. / There is more than one road" (3).

—*Karis Shearer*

Notes

1 "Mackerel crowded seas": a reference to Yeats's "Sailing to Byzantium."
2 The response poem engages an earlier text, often parodying it and critiquing not only the content but also the form or genre. See Raleigh's "The Nymph's Reply to the Shepherd" in response to Marlowe's "The Passionate Shepherd to His Love"; Koch's "Variations on a Theme" in response to Williams's "This Is Just to Say"; and F.R. Scott's "All the Spikes But the Last" in response to Pratt's long poem *Towards the Last Spike*.

Works Cited

Arsenault, Jean. "Functional Poetry, Etc." *Delta* 9 (1959): 11–13.

Blaser, Robin. Introduction. *Infinite Worlds: The Poetry of Louis Dudek.* By Blaser. Montreal: Véhicule, 1988. 7–29.

Cohen, Leonard. Interview. Stromberg-Stein 95–96.

Davey, Frank. *Louis Dudek & Raymond Souster.* Vancouver: Douglas & McIntyre, 1980.

Dryden, John. *All for Love.* Ed. N.J. Andrew. London: New Mermaids, 1975.

Dudek, Louis. Letter to Ezra Pound. 12 November 1952. Pound mss. II. Lilly Library, Bloomington, IN.

———. *Atlantis.* Montreal: Delta, 1967.

———. "Beyond Autobiography." *Open Letter* 6.2–3 (Summer–Fall 1985): 107–14.

———. "A Note on Metrics." *Selected Essays and Criticism.* Ottawa: Tecumseh, 1978. 111–15.

———. "Patterns of Recent Canadian Poetry." *Selected Essays and Criticism.* Ottawa: Tecumseh, 1978. 94–110.

———. Preface. *Europe.* Erin, ON: Porcupine's Quill, 1991. 9–19.

Everson, Ron. Interview. Stromberg-Stein 97–101.

Gustafson, Ralph. Interview. Stromberg-Stein 103–106.

Jones, D.G. Interview. Stromberg-Stein 107–18.

Jonson, Ben. "*Timber, or Discoveries.*" Vol. 8 of *Collected Works.* Ed. C.H. Hereford Percy and Evelyn Simpson. 8 vols. Oxford: Clarendon Press, 1947.

Joyce, James. *A Portrait of the Artist as a Young Man.* 1916. New York: Viking, 1956.

Livesay, Dorothy. "Functional Poetry, Etc." *Delta* 9 (1959): 11–13.

MacDonald, Goodridge. "Functional Poetry, Etc." *Delta* 9 (1959): 11–13.

Mandel, Eli. "Functional Poetry, Etc." *Delta* 9 (1959): 11–13.

Nichol, bp. *The Martyrology: Book 5*. Toronto: Coach House, 1982.

Norris, Ken. Interview. Stromberg-Stein 119–22.

Pratt, E.J. *Towards the Last Spike*. *An Anthology of Canadian Literature in English*. Ed. Russell Brown, Donna Bennett, and Nathalie Cooke. Toronto: Oxford UP, 1990. 216–56.

Sánchez, Antonio Ruiz. *Travelling to Knowledge: An Essay on Louis Dudek's Long Poems*. Córdoba: Servicio de Publicaciones Universidad de Córdoba, 2005.

Schlegel, Friedrich. *Dialogue on Poetry and Literary Aphorisms*. Trans. Ernst Behler and Roman Struc. University Park, PA: Penn State UP, 1968.

Scott, Frank R. Interview. Stromberg-Stein 123–26.

Stromberg-Stein, Susan. *Louis Dudek: A Biographical Introduction to His Poetry*. Ottawa: Golden Dog, 1983.

Trehearne, Brian. *The Montreal Forties: Modernist Poetry in Transition*. Toronto: U of Toronto P, 1999.

Tremblay, Tony. "'a widening of the northern coterie': The Cross-Border Cultural Politics of Ezra Pound, Marshall McLuhan, and Louis Dudek." *The Canadian Modernists Meet*. Ed. Dean Irvine. Ottawa: U of Ottawa P, 2005. 153–77.

———. "'Git yr / eye off Canada / and onto internat criteria': Exploring the Influence of Ezra Pound on the Cultural Production of Louis Dudek." *Essays on Canadian Writing* 74 (Fall 2001): 26–52.

Yeats, William Butler. "Sailing to Byzantium." *Collected Poems*, 2nd ed. London: Macmillan, 1950. 217–18.

On Poetry and Profession

Functional Poetry: A Proposal

"Think of all the poems that have been written—"
No poems have yet been written!...
Written! They have been too much written.
But thought... the poems that are thought...
                    thought itself—
Think them!
They proceed... strips and pieces...
or whole clusters
as an apple branch proceeds
and the rain channeled
into the pip and skin and meat of apples

my branched thoughts proceed
dropping heavy apples,
                    bags of them,
as I accumulate that rain
for nectar, and the far far green
for the apple skins, and far whiter, the white for meat.

For some time now (since Whitman? since Lawrence?)
poets have been experimenting with
                    new subject matter, new forms
in the effort to break through an impasse.

The problem, it seems to me, is simply
the loss of ground to prose   over the centuries
in the subject matter of poetry,

and the loss of freshness in method
as the residue of "poetic" substance
became fossilized in decadent metre and form
                    —the coral reefs.

We want a renewal   of substance, of technique
                that goes to the origin and source:

To bring back current vigour, where refinement
        of aesthetic sensibility, and neglect (the push
of society in other directions) threatens poetry
                with virtual extinction.
                                        In Egypt
        "decorated pottery reached climaxes of achievement
        at an early stage and then faded away
        as man's energies were diverted into other lines"
                John A. Wilson, *The Culture of Ancient Egypt*

This may happen to us
        unless we show more enterprise and
invade the areas of life where human energy has gone.

As I understand it, this has been the objective
of all modernist experiment (in English
                since 1910, in French
        since Laforgue and Rimbaud at least)
Call it   a return to the parting of ways
                between poetry and prose.

We have been trying to win back lost ground

                                from prose.

Note first   the dullness of most recent poetry
                        even the best.
(Cf. "The New Laocoön," *Origin*, Spring 1956.) I've said in Delta 1
        we want poetry "as relevant and immediate as prose matter"

                                Imagine that
sniffed the doltish (as usual) Canadian Critic (Cogswell, in *Fiddlehead*)
        Poetry
                "as interesting as prose!"

But plodding prose
expository, endless, rhymeless prose
                    has won over poetry (since 1550 c.)
everything

of interest : story   (the novel) style (from Browne to James) drama
                    wisdom, reflection, psychology, good news
                        (emotion too! imagination too!)

while poetry is left (said Mallarmé)
with a void
                    an absence
                                        poverty—
a new religion, of beauty, in its pride
                    the essence of
                                        the greatest good!

            Chips tin-flash from the dull canal,
            a solid million, not one speck
                    but a split-second splash
            vanishing, as the axe of the sun
            shivers the grey lead level water:
            statistical, unexaminable, a surface
                    diamond and indestructible
            shines in the mind.

Perhaps.
But if so, poetry-religion's in a cul-de-sac,   has been
                    for three hundred years now
                                        like the amoeba
trying out new pseudo-podia
                    in the dark, with ever smaller
                                        effect.

                    Beauty
                        is
                      truth.

Your Metaphysical Poets
were not merely composing conceits
in which reason and emotion mix
                    (some new science, some
                            old faith)
but were "inspired by a philosophical conception
        like that of the *Divina Commedia*, the *De Rerum Natura*,
                        perhaps Goethe's *Faust*,
            and the role assigned to the human spirit
                    in the great drama of existence"
                            (Herbert Grierson)
i.e. capable of dealing with philosophical & metaphysical questions
                in the form of poetry.

What followed, Dryden— Pope—
was an overt effort to rescue
                poetry from sofa-stuffing rhetoric (e.g. blank verse
                    drama, epic)
and carry it over into prose
                        meaning!

Cut the poetry, they said
        at all costs, and get the lucid
        rational mind
                    on our side
                        Byron
was the last poet (except in Canada, some up to 1860)
            who defended the rational design.

The Romantics   gave that up.
They tried for the first time to lift poetry
        out into the circumambient sphere
dropping the ballast of reason, reality (prose matter)

and claiming vision, mystic
          revelation, sublimated
                    beauty in their palaces
of pure art —   sublimated verbiage
                              on a cosmic scale.

In that vein Coleridge
          Shelley (Prometheus) Poe
                    are familiar English
exponents of pure music (i.e. pure
                    of all save pure
                              nihilo)

and Mallarmé the master
                    of those who know
"nothing is poetry" in France, Greece (Seferis)
                    England, (CANADA), or USA.

Eliot said they (the Metaphysicals) were able to think
          in poetry—but he did not think.
Had (perhaps) thought: Wordsworth said
he also had thought: and he really thought
                              more than Eliot
in the poem—if only he had thought well!

To this, all our lines have been converging.

[*Pace* M. Benda: "les vertus intellectuals
                    n'ont rien à voir avec la poésie.]

I can hear Marianne Moore thinking—
                    her page
resembles functional speech
except that it is (as poetry) bad prose
One doesn't want to chase a rabbit
                    on snow shoes).

Williams of course
did the right thing, so far as rhythm and language
                    go
He simply did not have a lot (enough) to say.
        Williams is a joy
to read—the senses live
                    in his lines—the senses
are a good beginning
        with which to breach the wall
                            of prose.

Williams, Stevens, Cummings (in his variety), Pound
        (Pound, alas, in that he tried to ravage
                history & expose, & propagate
                        un-poetical emergency *idées fixes*
                            at all costs
            believing, alas, to the end   in music
                (pure) and in the aesthetic
                                    vacuum)

Auden (the public speech and thought return—
        as in Pope—but the metrics too—
                killing off the new shoots   of form)
Yeats, the middle phase, the conflict always
                in his aesthetic anti-modern pose.
Others   after Auden, Shapiro following
                    with a decasyllable *Essay on Rime*
Jeffers, with rhetorical intent
MacNiece in "Autumn Journal"
Frost in "New Hamphire"

But I go back always to the first free moderns
        Lawrence, Aldington, Eliot (then), Pound (1915)
                Lee Masters (yes! Sandburg too)
for the beginning of what we need: straight language
                and relevance to our real concerns

i.e. prose, an approach to prose
  "Chopped prose" is what they called
 vers libre in the beginning—
    "Listen to the fool's reproach
    IT IS A KINGLY TITLE!"

All these roads (of mod po)
converge in a single purpose
    to write it as they write prose
Lots of it, on all subjects that call
    for communication

Write whatever you write (for print, or letters)
  not as prose, but as rhythmic poetry
    (you will find the way)

(Why not "talk poetry," my friend Everson says
      amused)

i.e. some form of improvised rhythmed speech
which is divided and shaped
  by the run-on and end-stop system
      of notation.

poetry, instead of shapeless pouring prose, poetry ·
    having the shape of clouds.

In any case, I mean to do it
here for some time, writing prose
   articles and items
in this rhythm (or whatever I find)

as poetry of exposition and discourse
hoping to give a permanent shape
   to what is said   in the lines.

I am still my own delicious self

filled with love, filled with light
sitting in this hard chair, aware
of talk in the other room, that music,
        and the black shadows that play on the ceiling;
who drink in the world, the only true
world, that comes to me,
real though mortal—
a piece of whatever gods
        seeds and scouring stems
(or Gregory's eyelash—
    my new-created child)
possess—running a race with time…
A stone in a stream, washed clean
and standing, forever
        virginal
    as intelligent, imaginative man.

Theory of Art

In the wide circle of an eyeball
        at any moment
    the mind, or imagination, combines and recombines

windows and heads, a leaf and a cathedral,
        with unfailing unity,
    with a centre of interest, with an artist's iron will.

By the theory of optics, this *techne* is
        arrangement for
    the maximum of comprehension, to get in most of
                                    [a world—

miniscule cars at a distance and one's tree-sized finger
        perfectly fitted
    in the eyeball. And then you ask, "What does it mean?"

They say "the artist already tells you,
        and he does not know,"
    since there is more in this than meets the eye, and
                                    [comes

from "the greatest distance." His centre of interest
        is crossroads of the world:
    where in the round, as in an eyeball, we must stand,

a real thing, the human edifice, or shrink
        unmetamorphosed
    back into the empty eyepits of the skull.

"The poem is vision"—but think of that diagram
        of light coming to focus
    from all quarters, to the miniature in a pupil—

the whole world, there in compendium, all
        its huge fragments
    a silent landscape, in the perfect O of the eye!

What we Profess

In Greece it was a merchant
    who started a school of philosophy,
and a stonemason who taught Plato
    how to seek truth.

We who specialize in the discipline
    no longer know what we believe—

since those who teach know less than those who do.

Lesson

The poet says:
I exist only when you read me,
not when you praise.

You must read every line
         for the tremor
in every word, in every phrase.

I have been sent
     to bring you light,
the poet says.

It Is An Art

It is an art   observing
     "the truth of human experience"

Directly or indirectly—does it matter?

So today, the individual
         is at the heart of it
As in the past, some god
      some universal truth
         was the aim.

Today the individual is at the heart of it.
You yourself.

You are the subject of poetry.

Hellcats in Heaven

(Report on the book *Cerberus*)

François Villon read one half,
Ended with a bitter laugh:
"May you be hanged for this,"
He said. "It's awful stuff!"

Next to read was William Blake,
Said in a fit of coughing shakes:
"Will you build Jerusalem
With the boards of a jakes?"

Read it then, Arthur Rimbaud,
Read it shuddering as though
He had tasted something foul;
Then bawled "Merde—ça pue!"

Read it Maître Rabelais,
Laughed, but fell a-cursing too:
"'Tis true I said *faictz ce que veut*—
But how could I know what you would do?"

Kingston Conference

How green and cosy
        the campus looks,
         where the learned societies
meet, while atomic refuse is dumped into seas
      (already killed several species)

And life goes on so stupidly
        outside—commonplace, uneducated, real
menaced by great know-how, or ignored
         by scholars,
while the beautiful trees, placid and uninformed,
        look on.

Poetry Reading

I like to be at a meeting of poets
    where they read
Each proud of his art, stands up
and works his high effect

different from any other
                 strange, separate
as the grasses, or the species

Some declaim, others jest
some seem to suffer—for the sake of the game
    (as do all in fact)
some in the very clouds, some in dirt
but all devotional in their secular praise

of the actual and the endless ways
their syllables turn and return to contain themselves.

Line and Form

The great orchestrating principle of gravity
            makes such music of mountains
as shaped by the mathematical hands
      of four winds, clouds
           yield in excellent and experimental sculpture;
mushrooms, elephants
      and women's legs, have too their form
           generated within a three-dimensional space
             efficiently.

And so the emotions
      combine into exquisite
         counterparts of the mind and body
when the moving principle and the natural limits imposed
         work against each other,
           give in, and resist.

The form is then the single body
      of love that two wrestlers make.
But has each one his own?
           or is one?
What essential form has
        a wind or the sky
that cutting into each other
            they mimic living arms?
Eternal forms.
The single power, working alone
      rounds out a parabola
        that flies into the infinite;
but the deflected particle
        out of that line, will fetch a frisk
        of sixes and eights
          before it vanishes:

an ocean arrested
> by sudden solid
>> ripples out in the sand.

So this world of forms, having no scope for eternity,
> is created
in the limitation of what would be complete and
> perfect,
achieving virtue only
> by the justness of its compromises.

"Europe" at Sea

"You made it too long," said Michael
(the passages that say everything, he wanted).
"Too short," said Pratt.

"Not enough … Too much!" Some admired it.

One said, "The sea is great."
Another, "The Greeks."
"In France," a third, "you said most about the arts."

"I almost gave up in disgust
when I saw what you said about France,"
            wrote a fourth.

Some admired it.

"You couldn't add or subtract a word,"
writes the perfect friend.

Poetry

All writing is a distillation, from the life to the work, but poetry especially is a distillation: out of much verbiage and stupidity, to refine an image of the seraphic sage; or more simply, to find a voice, lost in the clutter and noise of existence, which speaks with perfect clarity, with simplicity, out of the true self.

Advice to a Young Poet

Your genius is hidden from you. You belch, you fart, you utter stupidities: gradually you eliminate these as not relevant to what you have to do. Discover where your real power lies. It is yours. Slowly you must bring out the hidden character of your work and discover yourself. Do not worry about weaknesses that must of themselves fall away. Look for the essential that is yours. Become original in this slow self-defining way.

And remember, there is no sudden reward. Publication through established presses is vanity. These are the real vanity presses. It is humility to publish privately, at your own cost.

The Retired Professor

I lecture in my dreams—a retired man
for whom life is one unending coffee break!

Death, interesting as a postman,
comes walking down my street of days.

Old Books

Our dear failed poems of long ago—

    Trio, and *Unit of Five*,
    and *Three Early poems of Lower Canada*...

We all have them, or books like them,
    shyly hidden on the back shelves,
        or just forgotten,
like the party dresses of youth
        no longer in fashion.

While new poets try their turn—
    Roo Borson's lovely lines,
    Sonja full of jive,
    and Ken, unhappy but still alive.
We love them, though the public
        prefers the ghost of Presley
and worships that fat calf.

So again the little books will gather
        later to raise a cloud
of dust when you breathe, or bring the tears to your eyes.

Dedications and Intertexts

For E.P.

For Christ's sake, you didn't invent sunlight;
There was sun dazzle before you, and stricken leaves,
Phoibus of the goddamned "narrow thighs"—
But you talk as if you made light or discovered it.

Kosmos: The Greek World

(*For Michael Lekakis*)

One day man opened his eyes and the sun blew
over his wet eyeballs a coloured flower—
kosmos of combed fields
       and valleys where cattle grazed;
the hills folded in equations, and streams
bubbled mathematically to the sea; even the sea
strident, went silent,
       counted to ten and reined in;
and thunder gulped its peal.
       What memory of pain
he then denied, fought, shut his eyes to,
       or reconciled,
to make that intellectual gain! But he did.
It may be he mastered himself just then; or maybe
it was the blue Mediterranean dazed him
to think death is gay.
       Yet he found everything to praise.
God rose on the face of the waters I think that day
and smiled, his first recognition to clay.

Emily Dickinson

I saw an oak tree in a pot,
    It was a very pretty thing:
Its branches had been often cut
    So that it kept its tiny plot.

The narrow body twisted up
    And glistened in the frightening sun;
Two feet of stem inside a cup—
    And yet an oak from root to top.

Nature is great in filling space
    Tight as an atom with desire,
But for a tree a room's no place;
    To put it there was a disgrace.

James Reaney's Dream Inside a Dream, or The Freudian Wish

I dreamed that my grandmother
gave birth to a grandfather clock
and out of the clock came my grandfather
and in his hand was my jock;
and I awoke out of his dream
and dreamed I was putting on my sock
when out of the sock came my grandmother
holding my grandfather's jock;
and I awoke out of this dream
and found myself in my socks
under the grandfather clock,
and in my hand was *my* jock.

Irving Layton's Poem in Early Spring

My friends, the people are devouring each other.
They will finish me off soon
with a gorgeous icepick.

They are mephitic as fly dung on cherry-stones.

But these pregnant buds opening like your
              genitals,
Are beautiful, dear, and swollen with greatness
Like my poems.

Rich Man's Paradise

(After F.R. Scott)

Behold these happy children at the Laurentian spa
Playing the juke box and drinking Coca-Cola:
Yet they must return to Lagauchetière Street
    After this little treat
To waste their stunted, unprofitable lives
For the profit of the few, under what we persist in calling
    "The System of Free Enterprise"!

Quebec Religious Hospital
by A.M. Klein

Scarp Aesculapian, promontorious embole,
Refluct and invert of populous teleopaths.
My youth's diagony, jejeune floraison,
I bow to you crutchless, in memory's name...

(*unfinished*)

Carman's Last Home

In "Sunshine House" lived Mrs. King
Where Carman with a turquoise ring
Dangled the bell, and often stayed,
Talked and sang, and wept and prayed.

At "Moonshine" on a summer's day
They danced in sandals — the Delsarte way —
While Unitrinian silence made
Their sorrows one, their joys a shade.

In "Ghost House" stayed eternal Bliss,
Melancholy, despite all this:
Sang of pure Love, and the Mystic One,
Wore his hair long, his tie undone.

They have passed on, and "Sunshine" too,
As all great luminaries do:
A Ryerson Chapbook contains the man
Of Vagabondia and the Pipes of Pan.

Europe Without Baedecker
But *with* Pound

"The cakeshops in the Nevsky"!!
...Now here's a copy of Fracastoro's *Syphilis*
and Heywood's *Mayden-head Well Lost*...

Envy? They say Addison found six fingers
on a hand in one of Veronese's best pictures
And Tasso, in a rage, they say, of envy
tore out the pages
  of Ariosto with his teeth.

Je t'ai vu dans "Les Parapluies" de Renoir
...like Van Eyck, did the heads magnificently
but failed with the simple apples.

One of a democracy
  of artists.

As for Usura,
see the portrait of Asher Wertheimer
  (by Sargent)
Museums, attics of civilization...

Tar and Feathers

Layton, we write our clabbered verses,
Yours a long catalogue of curses,
Mine one pure curse the song traverses—
And yet the fact's we both know what
We're cursing isn't worth a futt.
Old Ez advises "build a sewer"
When culture's gone into manure;
Mistaking his advice at times
We make a sewer of our rhymes.
Of course, the Montrealers' lives
Are dismal—they deserve their wives—
Of course the poems in the *Star*
Are worse than yours and mine, by far.
And Westmount's cultured smell is spoil
Refined from Point St. Charles's oil.
Sure what they read and what they think,
And say, gives off an awful stink.
The soda fountain "five-foot shelf"
Would have choked Gutenberg himself;
The stomach turns from what they feed
Their young, like sparrows, true indeed.
And yet, we itch to double-kill
What there is left half-living still.
Think of the mountain how it stands
And doesn't give a damn what cans,
Cupcakes and condoms people throw
Over its calm Shakespearean brow.
There will be time yet, mountains think,
To wash all cities down the sink.
That's how I'd like to stand at last,
If lust or inspiration last.
Here by the Fount of Youth, it's warm,
Coffee and pie need no reform,
The waitress makes quick verses come.

Teenagers crowd around the rack
Of sex and crime, but stay intact.
To pin-ball magic eyeballs roll,
The Farmby Program fills the soul,
Telling the folks how many cows
Were burned last night while chewing chows,
Who had a birthday, who ate hash
And died of piles in St. Eustache…
And shall we curse the cook who makes
The pink floss on the Pom-Pom cakes?
Or bend to mop the floor with poems
They'll hang to drip in all good homes?
Such choices still defeat our ends;
It's waste of time that passion spends,
For dead men all know something worse
Than still to be alive to curse!
The young are coming, whistling songs,
And we shall go like dinner gongs,
But Montreal will have its fleas
Though what you write "to teach and please"
Is swelling notes for Ph.D.'s.

The waitress asks me, "Something else, sir?"
"No, thanks." For this, no Bromo Seltzer.

Reply to Envious Arthur

Hail Coprophilia, muse of Layton, hail!
Doxy of Dudek skoal! who drop'st in pail
Thick streaming words and brownish lumps of rhyme—
Manure essential in this barren clime,
Where Saxon critics without guts or gall
Praise these thy sons but little, if at all.
Yet these are they who vindicate thy cause,
Who preach thy gospel and affirm thy laws:
Blest pair of poets, put on earth by thee
To sweat and strain and groan to set us free
From Anglo-philistine hypocrisy.
What shovelfuls of praise we ought to pay
These swart forerunners of an Augean day
Let us with candour, clangour, and no taste,
Make haste to proffer, oh make haste, make haste!
Layton shall how to flatter Layton teach,
And modest Dudek Dudek's glories preach:
Layton shall tingle in Canadian air,
And echo answer *Dudek* everywhere;
In ev'ry quarterly and magazine
Their linked names in squibs and puffs be seen;
Letters to editors be filled with them,
And gratitude replace each critic's phlegm:
Repentant Wilson, Smith, MacLure, and Frye
Shall who can praise than, loudest longest, try.

A.J.M. Smith, *The Canadian Forum*, May, 1957

It's little cause, Arthur, you have to complain
That I, or that my friend, may sometimes gain
A cough, or even applause, when we appear
To shout into the thick Canadian ear.
The nation being deaf to poetry, you know,
We're heard in London or Lansing, but not in Sault.
But you lack recognition for your pains
In whispering over the last cold remains
Of your own talent, or for Scott and Klein.
So naturally you resent *our* doing fine.

Remember there were times when you yourself
Were not above impacting critic's pelf.
Before your first, best, gifts forsook you
Before you'd published any book you
Had old Professor Collin sing hosannas
To you, in his windy *White Savannahs.*
Some six years later, bringing out your thin
First volume—how you took the critics in!
Almost posthumously, it might be said,
Since as a poet you were good as dead:
News of the Phoenix—as if any news
You brought was ever novel to the Muse!
You 'scaped the country after this affair;
Then from a cloud, or from a college chair,
You wrote, in ignorance, of "traditions," "trends,"
"The Cosmopolitan," "The Native"—nonsense without end.
At last, anthologizing others' wares,
Your own name grew on theirs, so it appears,
Till forc'd to publish or renounce your fame
You brought *A Sort of Ecstasy* out—a sort of lame
Last book, stuffed with discarded rhymes
That even our critics could not praise this time.
(Some of the poems were so little new
They came out of a 1928 Review;
And not a poem but was cribbed, 'tis said,
From Yeats, Pound, Auden, or the greater dead.)
The critics shook their heads, admired your skill
In writing nothing, and yet publishing still.
Ah well, you've always aimed at verse, we know.
So fine, by dint of labour labour would not show;
But in your own smooth lines, for lack of pith,
Only the labour shines—no genius, Smith!
Give over, then; and give up envy, man;
Let others win applause, or steal renown.
There's little glory, even for men like us,
Who've genius without labour, without fuss.

The Progress of Satire

(*For F.R. Scott and A.J.M. Smith*)

Reading a dead poet
Who complained in his time
Against bad laws, bad manners,
And bad weather in bad rhyme,

I thought how glad he'd be
To be living in our time
To damn worse laws, worse manners,
And worse weather, in worse rhyme.

The Demolitions
(*For John Glassco*)

The biggest name in Montreal these days is Teperman.
It stands a yard high, in front of old buildings:

```
TEPERMAN
Demolition
```

Teperman is working hard. I've seen the remains
of old dilapidated lovely city sections
                              go down in rubble—
"No Parking" signs over the lot.
And the whole city, including Cathedrals,
skyscrapers, the statue of Burns,
                    and our three universities,
level like these lots, as they will be ...

Teperman works fast. What does he care
whether any building we want to stand
                    for eternity goes?

His business is DEMOLITION
                    and swinging metal balls.

II

The block on Stanley (I've got to check with the street post)
where our bohemia was just commencing
                    and the beatnik gallery burned
where Leonard had his rooms (offered in friendship
                    to MM CD and others)
where the Riviera coffee house and the tenements and
          Betty's "Tailor"
                              had their domicile
where Sutherland set up the First Statement

and we read the poem by Souster, in manuscript,
                              "The Groundhog"
and Madame No-wee-jee-ess-ka carried on ...

So picturesque
            so picaresque
                        so European

Like the ruins of Warsaw, our only Latin Quarter
has been razed to the ground

I look at the empty space, and think of all the Hungarians
locked out in the world ...

                    III

The new buildings that rise on the rubble
                in flocks, to the langorous clouds,
will stand all night in their stories of light
                        swinging a searchlight to fear

but will not remember the slums
                at the roots of their bones
nor the dead who went down on a Stryker frame
nor the unfledged young
                    who disappear.

Lonely for new glory they wait
            for long leaseholds and the penthouse dwellers,
their corridors filled with maidens
                too simple to love, and too ignorant to care.

A Note for Leonard Cohen

To borrow vine leaves
pay for books ...
(awaken, world of memory)
By a field of timothy,
a stream for perch fishing,
with overhanging boughs ...
There we sat, the cyclists of those days:
And now you smile, all literature,
our *yong Squyer*,
whose poems are as good as ours
ever were!
Are we to rejoice, in you,
warming our cooled marrow juices
by what you say?
Or, as you imagine, be young with you?
Or call age, a new
kind of power—
an authority over joy?
Nuts, to all that!
You may be free, of us, be perfect
pitiful, without a thought, as we
will look here and there
for such crumbs as still
half satisfy: but you are
ourselves, and suffer the same brief
no, no more—the whole story
takes in the lot of us.

Tao

(*For F.R.S.*)

Things that are blown or carried by a stream
seem to be living—not in that they oppose the wind
or oppose the water, but in that they move
                                    lightly blown,
lightly flowing, like things that live.

We who are actually living do best when we do not resist,
    do not insist, when winds and waters blow,
but go gently with them, being of their kind,
in the secret of the wind and water, the thought of flow.

For Ron Everson

(After Ezra Pound, and Confucius)

To love one's friends who make poems,
     is not that happiness?
To have them come from far places
'back to the same old restaurant
        to read their six-line epics —
what could be more delightful?

Proust

It may be God takes such honey out of time
as bees from flowers —

the remembered sweet-cake and a view
of church spires.

Homosexuality

If you think homosexuality is a perversion, an abnormality in nature, then you will have very great difficulty in acknowledging some great artists as representatives of humanity: Leonardo da Vinci, Michelangelo, Shakespeare, Walt Whitman, André Gide, Marcel Proust, Oscar Wilde, E.M. Forster, Somerset Maugham, Hart Crane, W.H. Auden, Tennessee Williams, Jean Cocteau, Allen Ginsberg, Gore Vidal and many others.

A total change in our social and moral attitudes to homosexuality is certainly due, and it is much to be desired. First there is the benefit of justice to those who happen to be homosexual, both men and women; and then there is the great change in society that this will bring—like opening wide windows and letting in light and air— when the energies that are now concealed and lurking in the dark have full play and intermingle with the heterosexual reality that we have channelled too narrowly.

For William Carlos Williams

O hell, did you have to do it
                                        now, Bill
when we were just getting
the whiplash of your New Measure, crack
                of words in the sun, over the woman eating
plums, over the burning greens?

When we were getting the hang of it, to your glory,
                and bringing the baskets home,
stuff you planted in your Earlier and Later
                                        Collected Poems

praising the world
                and talking to the cabman
about "Pound and economics" so many beginnings

Those forceps, stethoscopes (the way to their hearts)
and medical books you could never keep up with
                —thrown away, finished?

Isn't it (death) stupid? That all a man is,
                those immediate moments
you tried to cling to, should be thought "ephemeral"?

Death is a liar, Bill Williams   Don't think for a minute
                that we believe him   It's all the same
It's as you said, every minute of it, here, now, real and forever.

Long Poems

From *Europe*

95

The sea retains such images
　　　in her ever-unchanging waves;
for all her infinite variety, and the forms,
inexhaustible, of her loves,
she is constant always in beauty,
　　　which to us need be nothing more
　　　than a harmony with the wave on which we move.
All ugliness is a distortion
of the lovely lines and curves
　　　which sincerity makes out of hands
　　　and bodies moving in air.
Beauty is ordered in nature
　　　as the wind and sea
shape each other for pleasure; as the just
know, who learn of happiness
　　　from the report of their own actions.

From *En México*

Do the arts matter?
As tourist fodder,
      as the rich man's grovel.
From a beginning of adobe huts
and jungle kraals…

We have been in the place where hurricanes begin
with hot sidereal spin,
taking their rise from the turbulence of the water,

and the dusty horizon
a dream of distance,
of silence…
then a sudden roar.

Among the ruins of blood-hungry gods.

Cortésian enterprise
turned a continent to a tornado
from this silver spout:
his loot, the jewelry of the cheap stores!

Cortés died old and poor
who was the young Alexander.

      . . .

It is most quiet
where it is most violent.
That's why we appear so good.

In a tropical cemetery
hardly a grave is to be seen,
so much is overgrown.

And where Cortés with his men
(their pockets full of booty)
waded in blood, they've drained
the lake and streetcars ride
where he shook the Indian by the arm and cried,
        "You have destroyed
the most beautiful city in the world —
                Tenochtitlan!"

He opened the continent
        like a cornucopia.

        . . .

Mejicano, mestizo,
have got religion up to the gills:
conferred on them by the Spaniards
to give enslavement a proper face.

Language. Silence
        is also a language.
When there is no order in heaven,
we make what we make
by luck, or strength,
or the composition of desire.
Power grows
        like vegetation.
There are no preferences under heaven.
And I do not know why a leaf should be of less worth
        than a Vatican
or why builders care;
but the mathematical stones recite their logic
of cruelty and despair:
we arose to gratify the reason
shaping the empty air.

        . . .

Religion,
         always used
to put a safe stamp on terror.
First the enemy one hates
              is "sacrificed"
then one's own kind.
To contain fear, in ignorance;
in our time weakness, insecurity, mental pain.

They say no more, as language
                        (art, or faith)
than any other language;
speak as leaves do,
as dogs sniffing,
as the mating glow-worm sending a call.

And may be wrong.
We make advances
         toward humility.

You may hate the jungle,
its inimical insects, flies,
and the chaos of growing
everything at once;
but we return for fertility
to its moist limbs
and vaginal leaves.

They grow over each other, overgrow,
and the whole thing, by elimination,
is also an order that exists.
Hence the necessary magnificence of all reality.

(Where an artist is only a pipsqueak
in a forest of mocking birds.)

So praise the glory of the green jungle
with all its terrible thunder;
praise death and generation
and the embracement of lovers under all skies.
Praise frost and thaw, and the congealing of
                                        elements,
or their prismatic flow;
      praise the disposition of ferns,
and the erection of great trees.
Praise hovels and giant domes
and the ant's most secular mound.
Between cathedral spires
and the plum tree's pleasantness
there is no distinction.
Praise these.

            . . .

Mexico, strange suffering land:
lazy, inflammable,
      lacking the meanest comforts.

Dragging their degradations like any people
who have suffered from much rapacity
through generations:
in rotting straw, eating offal,
serving now the power of cold machines.

(Till the guiltiness of an action
is itself the motive for it,
so far have our pleasures
been bred to our guilts.)

Americans enjoying
the benefits of their poverty and cheap labour.

We learn the rudiments here,
coming only for play.

Removed by guilt from oppression,
by rest from our proper fray.

. . .

Study the way of breaking waves
for the shape of ferns,
                    fire and wind
for whatever blows or burns.

Someday we shall come again to the poem
as mysterious as these trees,
                    of various texture,
leaves, bark, fruit
(the razor teeth so neatly arranged,
so clean the weathered root).
There is an art of formal repetition
and the art of singular form—lines, lines
          like a wave-worn stone.

Afterword

"All these roads"—the phrase not only accurately notes the numerous journeys any editor of Louis Dudek's poetry must undertake but also the persistently divergent and intertextual quality of both Dudek's writings and literary life. When Dudek encountered roads that diverged—in woods of any colour—it did not occur to him that one road necessarily could be not taken. In his writing generally, in individual books, and in his little magazine *Delta* he would frequently take not only several roads but several of them contemporaneously. In *Delta* he placed poems by himself and others alongside his editorials and his notes on his readings in the sciences and social sciences. He wrote the witty and often tightly versified satires of *Laughing Stalks* in the same years that he was writing the expansive and intricately layered long poems *Europe* and *En México*—a period in which he was also teaching modernist literature at McGill, helping edit poetry and publish it at Contact Press, and writing numerous essays, including his important historicizing ones on Lampman, Carman, Roberts, and Pratt.

Moreover, the road of poetry for Dudek was broad, and could take one almost anywhere. As Karis Shearer notes here in her introduction, Dudek deplored the narrowing of poetry's functions that had occurred in the nineteenth and early twentieth century with such concepts as "art for art's sake" and the New Criticism's "autotelic" poetry; he deplored equally the more recent reduction of poetry to entertainment or stand-up comedy that he believed had occurred in the work of Leonard Cohen and Irving Layton. Poetry for Dudek should be a genre in which the major issues of the time are engaged, a genre that encourages reflection among influential readers, and has determinative effect on both private life and public policy. He worked to increase both the intellectual focus of poetry and its public circulation.

Dudek's background as the son of working-class Polish immigrants contributed enormously to the gifts he could give a Canadian literature that had been until his time overwhelmingly anglophile. In all of his writings Dudek instinctively saw his literary inheritance as Euro–North American rather than British or Anglo-American. His major books would include a *Europe*, an *En México*, and an *Atlantis*, but nothing resembling a *Dunkirk*, *Titanic*, or *Strait of Anian*. Critics who have positioned Dudek's poetry within an assumed

conflict between British and North American poetics overlook this compli-
cation. His sense of writing within a Euro–North American context was, if
anything, strengthened by his literary friendship with Ezra Pound, whose
own perspectives were distinctly European. Dudek's work, along with that of
contemporaries such as Klein, Waddington, Layton, Grove, and Marlyn, thus
points to a still mostly unacknowledged multiculturalism in mid-twentieth-
century Canada that profoundly enlarged literary and cultural possibility.
Efforts to study recent multiracial multiculturalism in Canadian writing
would benefit from a recognition that multiculturalism in Canada, and
clashes and collisions between different cultural inheritances and metaphor-
ically "diasporic" migrations, long predate the invention of that controversial
m-word. The reception of Dudek's writing—the hostility of Frye, the reser-
vations of Smith, the indifference of many scholars even before Goldie[1]—
was troubled in part because that writing was to a large extent inspired by
"foreign" or international modernist understandings of the literary and of
literary labour. Similar reception of writers such as NourbeSe Philip, Marilyn
Dumont, or Roy Miki may be new and surprising to contemporary critics,
but they are not at all new to Canada.

   When in Vancouver at the end of the 1950s I first became aware of Dudek's
various projects it was this difference—from both the established anglocentric
Canadian poetries that acknowledged Yeats, Auden, Thomas, and Barker and
the conflicting often nationalist preoccupations of the various US poetries—
that was most apparent. The field of reference of his work seemed cosmopoli-
tan—we might now say metropolitan. Yet he was an outsider, from Montreal
rather than Toronto—and outside the Canadian club of prize-winning poets.
His little magazine *Delta* seemed like a workplace for poetry and ideas, in
contrast to the display-case for Literature that the better-financed *Tamarack
Review* appeared to be. What was most interesting to me about Dudek were
the models he offered for broadening poetry into the seemingly nonliterary,
i.e., into arenas of cultural engagement, and for getting new poetry published
and distributed inexpensively but effectively. When he happened to be hired
to teach a senior poetry workshop at the University of British Columbia in
the summer of 1962, I enrolled—and was surprised to encounter a Creative
Writing course with a final examination. It wasn't just in his reviews and
essays that Dudek demanded that poets be knowledgeable about contem-
porary poetry and its history; he expected this also of his poetry students—
an understanding of the history of English-language poetics, of traditional
prosody and poetic forms, of literary activism, of the principles of various
European modernisms. He expected novice poets to know and understand
the larger literary cultures they aspired to enter and alter—an expectation

which could be a shock to a student who writes from a simple aesthetics of lyric innocence. They needed such knowledge so that they could intelligently situate their own writing and understand its intertextual resonances—so that they could make informed differences.

I realized later that one of the reasons Dudek had come to Vancouver that summer was to meet me and George Bowering, Fred Wah, Jamie Reid, and the other young writers associated with the monthly poetry newsletter *Tish*, which we had launched the previous September. Perhaps he had recognized that one of the models for *Tish*, along with Cid Corman's *Origin* and LeRoy Jones's and Diane di Prima's *The Floating Bear*, was his *Delta*. But the very fact that he had troubled to come was significant, and connects to Leonard Cohen's remark, cited here by Shearer, about Dudek's "sense of responsibility." This was a responsibility not—as it has been for many poets—to oneself and one's personal "Art" or career, but to poetry as a material field, and to the ongoing construction of poetry in Canada. I suspect he had come to make us feel welcome in poetry in Canada—and in the radical European modernist traditions he had been trying to make a part of Canadian poetry (and that were somewhat present already—from Pound through Robert Duncan—in our own writing). Dudek's interest was, one might say, "functional" as well as generous. Within two months of the end of that course he had published the "New Vancouver Poetry" issue of *Delta*, with an introduction written by myself, and poems by me, Bowering, Reid, R.S. ("Red") Lane, David Bromige, Lionel Kearns, Wayson Choy, John Newlove, and Phyllis Webb.

There have not been many close ties between generations in Canadian poetry. While there have been shared thematic interests—D.M.R. Bentley argues, for example, that "early long poems on Canada occur at the intersection of Canadian subject-matter and a variety of imported forms and genres" fashionable at the time[2]—most poets have chosen to work not by modifying the forms of earlier Canadian poets but by reworking those of non-Canadian contemporaries. Many well-regarded Canadian poets of the present give the impression that they have had no interest in reading the poetry of any earlier Canadians—that is, that they do not regard them as precursors. This cavalier attitude toward the Canadian past has been due partly to the arrogance bred by the continuing Romantic myth of poetic originality, partly to the emphasis on self-expression and self-representation that identity politics has bred, and partly also to the contemporary emphasis on race and ethnicity and the false assumption that often accompanies this that cultural work from outside such categories is of dubious relevance. If alive today, Dudek would have been as interested in reading the poetry of Rita Wong or Erin Moure as he had been in reading that of Lionel Kearns, Wayson Choy, Gwendolyn MacEwen, or

Margaret Atwood in the 1960s, even though he might not admire it or envy the writing of it. "You can't edit what you don't admire," he wrote to Raymond Souster in 1966 when they discussing the disbanding of Contact Press, but he had continued to read and intellectually engage what he didn't admire—as he had read and engaged the poetry of D.C. Scott, Roberts, Carman, Pratt, Smith, and F.R. Scott. It is evident in the long interview that George Bowering, Steve McCaffery, bpNichol and I conducted with him in the fall of 1980 that he has serious reservations about some of the writing of his interviewers; but it is also evident that he could respect and discuss what he did not admire, much as we could respect with reservation his own poetry and cultural positions. Moreover, one of the reasons this interview was occurring was that Dudek had given *Delta* and Contact Press to Canadian poetry, beginning a chain of events in which Dudek would teach at UBC in 1962; Bowering, Newlove, and I would publish books with Contact Press; Daphne Marlatt, James Reid, Robert Hogg, Fred Wah, Victor Coleman, Michael Ondaatje, David McFadden, and bp Nichol would be included in the last Contact Press book; Raymond Souster would publish his poetry anthology *New Wave Canada*; Ondaatje would publish his *Long Poem Anthology* in 1979; and I would publish my study *Louis Dudek & Raymond Souster* in 1980.

One of the lessons of Dudek's career is that "Canadian" has been a somewhat floating and flexible signifier for a very long time. As I have observed numerous times, "Canadian" is constituted by the accumulating activities of those who self-identify as Canadians.[3] It is not an ideal rooted in eighteenth-century events, as Grant or Mathews would have us believe, or an ahistorical "theme" as Frye, Jones, and Atwood once proposed. This is why beliefs that earlier Canadian writing is irrelevant to present-day writers are ill founded. This is also why assertions that globalization's pressures are bringing about an "unravelling of the [Canadian] nation's coherence," resulting in "a loss of purpose," such as those made by the organizers of the 2005 TransCanadas conference, can seem so naive—or Macchiavellian. There has never been a stable coherent Canada; it has since colonial times been under (re)negotiation. Irish immigrants in the nineteenth century and eastern and southern European and Jewish immigrants in the first half of the twentieth were greeted with as much fear, suspicion, and bigotry, and subject to as much isolation, as black and Asian immigrants are today. They were even "racialized" as "black" or "dark" or "swarthy" in the same rhetoric that reached its extreme form in 1930s Germany. That is, they were constructed as nearly as "visible" through their appearance and "odd" names as were early black and Asian immigrants. Their intermarriage with British-descended Canadians, as Ralph Connor's *The Foreigner* (published in 1909, only nine years before Dudek's birth) problematically shows, was more controversial than so-called "mixed-race" marriages are today.[4] Dudek's fellow Montreal poet Irving Layton—like numerous other early twentieth-century Canadian members of families that had emigrated from eastern Europe—saw it advisable in 1937 to anglicize his name.

Normalizing such negotiations by pretending that they occurred within a "white" dominant constituency, as recent discourses have done that have opposed people "of colour" with those presumably of no colour, risks simplifying Canadian history and obliging us to re-understand cultural processes we should have already at least partly understood. Visibility and bigotry have degrees. Race and colour are culturally constructed categories. Louis Dudek is—along with Klein and Layton—part of the first group of non-British-Isles-descended poets to achieve prominence in Canada. He engaged but did not assimilate to the acknowledged poetries of mid-twentieth-century Canada, instead returning again and again—poetically and literally—to Europe for ways of fashioning a more public, discursive, and idea-oriented Canadian poetry than ever became acceptable to Canada's literary gatekeepers during his lifetime. He enlarged Canadian poetry by contributing further differences. That he was accorded few official honours—an FRSC, but never a Governor General's, an Order of Canada, or a Molson—reflects less on him than on the quality of the awards and the ability of those who give them to identify historically consequential cultural work.

—*Frank Davey*

Notes

1 See Shearer's introduction, p. xv.
2 *Mimic Fires: Accounts of Early Long Poems on Canada* (Kingston and Montreal: McGill-Queen's University Press, 1995), 308.
3 Globalization, unless it were to lead to the elimination of nation-states—something most observers currently believe unlikely (it is presently founded on relations among nation-states)—is not going to significantly alter this ongoing construction of a nation.
4 See the September 2007 CBC feature (www.cbc.ca/news/background/mixedblessings/) on the 35 percent increase in "mixed-race" marriages in Canada between the 1996 and 2001 censuses, and the wide news coverage the program received.

Acknowledgements

The editors and the publisher gratefully acknowledge Gregory Dudek for his permission to reprint the poems listed below. The lines by A.J.M. Smith on page 38 are reprinted with the permission of William Toye, literary executor of the estate of A.J.M. Smith.

From *Delta*
  "Functional Poetry"

From *The Searching Image* (Toronto: Ryerson Press, 1952)
  Line and Form

From *Cerberus* (Contact Press, 1952)
  For E.P.

From *Europe* (Laocoon Press, 1954)
  Fragment 95

From *Transparent Sea* (Contact Press, 1956)
  Theory of Art
  Kosmos: The Greek World (*For Michael Lekakis*)
  Emily Dickinson

From *En México* (Contact Press, 1958)

From *Laughing Stalks* (Contact Press, 1958)
  Hellcats in Heaven (Report on the book *Cerberus*)
  James Reaney's Dream Inside a Dream, or The Freudian Wish
  Irving Layton's Poem in Early Spring
  Rich Man's Paradise (*After F.R. Scott*)
  Quebec Religious Hospital by A.M. Klein
  Carman's Last Home
  Europe Without Baedeker But *with* Pound
  Tar and Feathers
  Reply to Envious Arthur
  The Progress of Satire (*For F.R. Scott and A.J.M. Smith*)
  "Europe" at Sea

From *Collected Poetry* (Delta Canada, 1971)
   The Demolitions (*For John Glassco*)

From *Cross-Section: Poems 1940–1980* (Coach House, 1980)
   Kingston Conference
   Poetry Reading
   A Note For Leonard Cohen
   Tao (*For F.R.S.*)

Ideas for Poetry (Véhicule, 1983)
   Poetry
   Advice to a Young Poet
   Homosexuality

From *Zembla's Rocks* (Véhicule, 1986)
   The Retired Professor
   For William Carlos Williams

From *Small Perfect Things* (DC Books, 1991)
   What we Profess
   For Ron Everson (After Ezra Pound, And Confucius)
   Proust

From *The Caged Tiger* (Empyreal, 1997)
   It Is An Art
   Lesson

From *The Surface of Time* (Empyreal, 2000)
   Old Books
   Letter to Ezra Pound, 12 November [1952], courtesy Lilly Library,
      Indiana University, Bloomington, IN

lps Books in the Laurier Poetry Series
Published by Wilfrid Laurier University Press

Di Brandt
Speaking of Power: The Poetry of Di Brandt by Di Brandt, edited by Tanis MacDonald, with an afterword by Di Brandt • 2006 • xvi + 56 pp. • ISBN-10: 0-88920-506-X; ISBN-13: 978-0-88920-506-2

Dennis Cooley
By Word of Mouth: The Poetry of Dennis Cooley by Dennis Cooley, edited by Nicole Markotić, with an afterword by Dennis Cooley • 2007 • xxii + 62 pp. • ISBN-10: 1-55458-007-2; ISBN-13: 978-1-55458-007-1

Lorna Crozier
Before the First Word: The Poetry of Lorna Crozier by Lorna Crozier, edited by Catherine Hunter, with an afterword by Lorna Crozier • 2005 • xviii + 62 pp. • ISBN-10: 0-88920-489-6; ISBN-13: 978-0-88920-489-8

Christopher Dewdney
Children of the Outer Dark: The Poetry of Christopher Dewdney by Christopher Dewdney, edited by Karl E. Jirgens, with an afterword by Christopher Dewdney • 2007 • xviii + 60 pp. • ISBN-10: 0-88920-515-9; ISBN-13: 978-0-88920-515-4

Don Domanski
Earthly Pages: The Poetry of Don Domanski by Don Domanski, edited by Brian Bartlett, with an afterword by Don Domanski • 2007 • xvi + 62 pp. • ISBN-10: 1-55458-008-0; ISBN-13: 978-1-55458-008-8

Louis Dudek
All These Roads: The Poetry of Louis Dudek by Louis Dudek, edited by Karis Shearer, with an afterword by Frank Davey • 2008 • xx+ 70 pp. • ISBN 978-1-55458-039-2

M. Travis Lane
The *Crisp Day Closing on My Hand: The Poetry of M. Travis Lane*, edited by Jeanette Lynes, with an afterword by M. Travis Lane • 2007 • xvi + 86 pp. • ISBN-10: 1-55458-025-0; ISBN-13: 978-1-55458-025-5

Tim Lilburn
Desire Never Leaves: The Poetry of Tim Lilburn by Tim Lilburn, edited by Alison Calder, with an afterword by Tim Lilburn • 2007 • xiv + 50 pp. • ISBN-10: 0-88920-514-0; ISBN-13: 978-0-88920-514-7

Don McKay
Field Marks: The Poetry of Don McKay by Don McKay, edited by Méira Cook, with an afterword by Don McKay • 2006 • xxvi + 60 pp. • ISBN-10: 0-88920-494-2; ISBN-13: 978-0-88920-494-2

Al Purdy
The More Easily Kept Illusions: The Poetry of Al Purdy by Al Purdy, edited by Robert Budde, with an afterword by Russell Brown • 2006 • xvi + 80 pp. • ISBN-10: 0-88920-490-X; ISBN-13: 978-0-88920-490-4